SCHOOL ON WHEELS

Reaching and Teaching
the Isolated Children of the North

At the Capreol station Fred Sloman talks with the railway men.

SCHOOL ON WHEELS

Reaching and Teaching
the Isolated Children of the North

◆ Karl and Mary Schuessler ◆

Canadian Cataloguing in Publication Data

Schuessler, Karl, 1929-
   School on wheels

ISBN 0-919783-46-5

1. Schools, Traveling - History.   2. Visiting
teachers - History.   3. Sloman family.
4. Education, Rural - Ontario - History.
5. Education of children - Ontario - History.
I. Schuessler, Mary, 1929-   .   II. Title.

LC5767.S35
1986   371'.01'097131   C86-093961-8

Published by:
THE BOSTON MILLS PRESS
132 Main Street
Erin, Ontario N0B 1T0
(519) 833-2407

Design by John Denison
Typeset by Fray & Young, Guelph
Printed by Ampersand, Guelph

We wish to acknowledge the financial
assistance and encouragement of The
Canada Council, the Ontario Arts Council
and the Office of the Secretary of State.

Publicity Photo of Gordon Pinsent in
"And Miles to Go".   - CBC TV drama   September 11, 1985

FOREWORD

The story of the railway school car keeps coming back.

Even though the last two cars finished their runs in 1967, their history continues to surface. As recently as last year Gordon Pinsent wrote and played the lead in the hour-long television drama "And Miles To Go," a fictionalized account of a troubled teacher who fled to the northern bushland of Ontario in an attempt to save both himself and his career.

No one watched the drama with more interest than Cela and Margaret Sloman of Clinton, Ontario. Cela Sloman lived the school car story with her husband Fred for thirty-nine years. Margaret grew up on the rail car, where her father taught her through Grade 12. The Sloman women agreed that Pinsent captured the beauty and isloation of the North Country and the "pure gold of the people, down to the last child." But the teacher he portrayed hardly represented the type of men they knew as school car teachers.

As part of his research for the story, Pinsent came to Clinton and visited the Slomans over a two-day period. In his TV role he wore a floppy brimmed hat, rubber galoshes on his feet and a pack over his back — all hallmarks of the late Fred Sloman.

When the school cars were in operation, many newspapers and magazines carried the story. Fred Sloman contributed a number of colourful accounts. Essays, university term papers and information from the publicity offices of the railroads told the school car story. Brief paragraphs appeared in books. This year Ted Ferguson's *Sentimental Journey, An Oral History of Train Travel in Canada* mentions the hospitable Slomans and their school car.

Eight years ago we traveled with a tape recorder through Ontario's North and recorded the memories of former school car teachers and students. The material became an hour-long documentary for the CBC radio network program "Between Ourselves."

In this book we have assembled all the scraps and snippets of the school car history into one account. Cela and Margaret Sloman continue to serve as the vast reservoir of information about life on the school car. They graciously shared hours and hours of their time. Another daughter, Fredda Rainey, better known as Toby, who lives nearby the family home, helped to gather material.

In 1984 Cela Sloman received from Governor-General Madame Jeanne Sauve in Ottawa the Order of Canada citation for her years of service on the school car.

Throughout this account the Slomans have served as the representative schoolteacher and family. Their story is duplicated in the lives of many other teachers and their wives.

Karl and Mary Jane Schuessler
March 2, 1986

The School Car Routes

(The routes changed over the years as enrollment rose and fell. Several of the cars' route numbers also changed as the school car service declined. Here is a list of the original car routes and the dates they began).

Canadian National

1926   CN School Car #1
Capreol to Foleyet
(The Sloman car)

1928   CN School Car #2
Port Arthur (Thunder Bay)
to Sioux Lookout

1930   CN School Car #3
Port Arthur (Thunder Bay)
to Fort Frances

1934   CN School Car #4
Sioux Lookout to the
Manitoba border

Canadian Pacific

1926   CP School Car #1
Cartier to Chapleau

1928   CP School Car #2
Fort William (Thunder Bay)
to Kenora

Temiskaming and Northern Ontario Railroad   (Now Ontario Northland)

1938   TNO School Car #1
North Bay to Cobalt

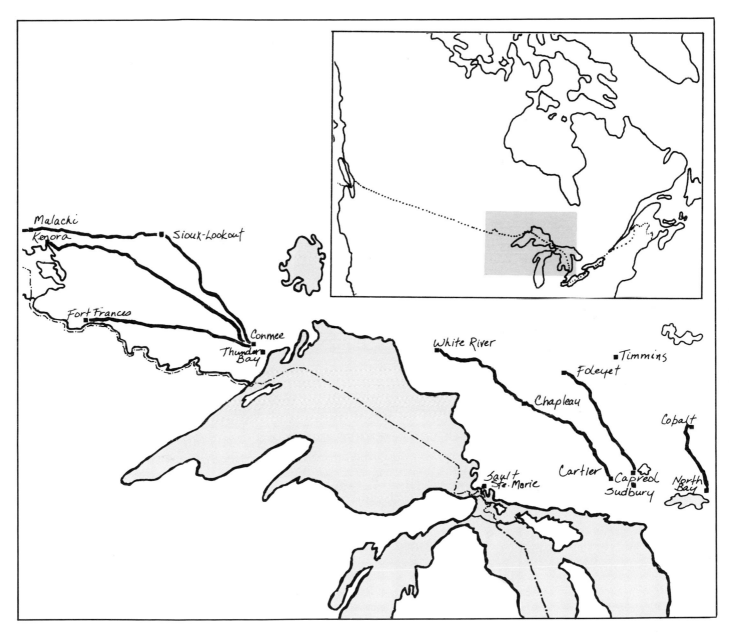

A map of the seven school car routes.

Fred Sloman shakes hands with his students at Kukatush, the next to the last stop on his line. On the platform stands Cela Sloman and their daughter, Joan.

"I had kids use fret saws ... and saw out letters to read Canadian National School-On-Wheels. And they were white washed and tacked to the car. Later the Shops in Capreol kindly painted the poorly cut letters in gold, and without any official sanction of the Department of Education or Railway, the name ... seemed to become official."

Fred Sloman

Fred and Cela Sloman sat in the school car and watched the lights of the Toronto Exhibition go out. The music and noise faded into the warm September evening as the 1926 Exhibition closed for another year.

"We were told we were going to leave that night," recalls Cela Sloman, "so I went down early with baby Joan and put her to bed in the school car." The couple drank a cup of coffee with Walter McNally, the other school car teacher. They said, "Goodbye."

For two weeks the two school cars, one Canadian National and the other Canadian Pacific, stood side by side on a track at the fairgrounds. Thousands of people flocked through to look at the newly outfitted cars made over into a combination schoolroom and living quarters. The Premier, G. Howard Ferguson, and officials of the Department of Education had paid a visit and made their inspection.

At midnight a steam engine moved in and coupled the Sloman car. They stood at the end of the car and waved at Walter McNally as an engine pulled his school car past them. Bachelor McNally was on his way to North Bay. His school car won the distinction of the first car on the rails. It beat out the Sloman rail car by fifteen minutes!

The engine moved the Slomans past the Exhibition buildings and the fairgrounds that sprawled along the edge of Lake Ontario's shores. It made a turn and headed north onto the tracks that led to Sudbury and the wilderness of rock and muskeg beyond.

The Slomans started to relax as their car rumbled through the night. Finally they were on their way! They had miles to go, of course, but they were off at last on this early September morning.

They knew their school car would stand on display for several more days in Sudbury. There they would greet visitors, give more guided tours and answer more questions. But now every belch of the steam from the engine and scream of the train's whistle brought them nearer to their destination.

Fred Sloman was about to take up his duties as teacher on a railroad car that would stand on a lonely siding for several days at a time. And by his side — or just through the narrow passageway into the living quarters — would be his wife Cela. When she married Fred, three years earlier, she had given up teaching kindergarten in Toronto. And now they were to take up this missionary-like adventure, to serve on the fringes and outposts of Northern

Ontario. But they knew this cooperative venture between the two railroads and Department of Education was only a six-month test run.

The Department had handpicked its first two teachers for this novel experiment in education. Both Fred Sloman and Walter McNally loved the North country. They had backwoods, one-room-school teaching experience. They shared the visionary dream of bringing education to the children of railroad men, trappers, miners, loggers, hunters and the native peoples. They accepted the challenge with enthusiasm, dedication and a spirit of self-sacrifice.

Interior view of living quarters in school car #15071

The Canadian National Railway Yards in Capreol, Ontario.

"As a returned soldier I got a nice job in a good school. But teaching Latin one day to one of the brightest classes I have ever seen, it seemed to me that these children would become lawyers, politicians and tycoons, with or without me to teach them. So I threw up my job and came to the bush."

Fred Sloman

After the Slomans stayed on the Sudbury track for two days of exhibition, a freight engine moved the car twenty-five miles further north to Capreol. That town, a railroad centre and divisional point, served as the southern starting point for their school car route.

The first day of instruction began at Nandair, a siding eight miles out of Capreol, on September 20, 1926. On hand stood the Slomans and the school inspector himself, J. B. MacDougall. They had set up the flagpole at the end of the car and hoisted high the Union Jack. The flag flying aloft — on that day and every day afterward — always signaled the start of a new school day.

A number of children and parents came up and gawked at the car. Up until that day only freight cars stood on the siding. The inspector and the Slomans welcomed the families. They noticed however that one family hung back. "I can remember it like yesterday," recalls Cela Sloman, who is now eighty-nine years old. "A mother and all her twenty-two children right down to the new baby stood there. Some of

the other children had told them they couldn't attend the school car, because their father wasn't a railroad man."

Inspector MacDougall asked Cela to assure the mother that her children were welcome. Everyone, including the trapper's family, climbed the steps and went into the school car. After the Slomans gave them a tour through the car, Fred wasted no time in enrolling his students. He taught them their first lesson.

J. B. MacDougall stayed on for the first few days at the Nandair stop. He was thrilled with the response. He reported that "everyone in the settlement stood about the car for a long time, inspecting it and admiring the equipment. They were happy in the thought that at last there were educational facilities provided for the children."

The inspector left the Slomans when they departed for their next stop at Antice. The success at the first station point repeated itself at every siding during that month. On October 25th the Slomans finished their first run between Capreol and Foleyet. Teacher McNally's school car had plied the rails between Cartier and Chapleau on the Canadian Pacific line.

After the first year's run, the two teachers reported that their school cars had served eighty-four children at fourteen separate points. Fifty-seven of the children had no previous schooling. Only four claimed English as their mother tongue.

For the next thirty-nine years the 148 miles

Fred Sloman with his students at Kukatush. He wears a pair of old army pants and puttees—wrappings for the legs to protect against the flies of summer and the cold of winter.

- CN Archives

between Capreol and Foleyet became Fred Sloman's schoolyard. The six-month experiment turned into his lifelong vocation. He became known as the Dean of the School Cars and the Dr. Livingston of the North. He was called missionary, humanitarian and a mender of broken hearts and bones.

He taught Grades 1 — or Primer, as it was then called — to Grade 13 or Fifth Form. He also taught a business course. On the school car, Fred and Cela raised their own five children. Cela became the gracious hostess to the Far North people. Over the years she served thousands of cups of coffee and baked millions of cookies. She became the friend, confidante and helper to the lonely women in the North.

Baby Joan with her railroad lantern. "She was just big enough to get up on the steps," says Cela.

"We will have to revise our idea of education. Two boys who could not write the word 'cat' when they came, wrote social letters after only 17 days of schooling."

Fred Sloman

The arrival of the school car made the Northland yield up its inhabitants. "We didn't know there were so many people in the bush," says Cela Sloman. "They seemed to come out from nowhere."

The students traveled on skis and snowshoes. They rode in on handcars. They walked on foot. They paddled in canoes. They came out of the little houses strung along the railroad tracks. Some traveled from as far away as twenty miles. They were all drawn to the school car, whose coal oil lamps blazed out into their dark world. "We had lots of light," says Cela Sloman. "Everyone loved to see the school car with its lights coming. When the sun went down, the little shacks had only one kerosene lamp on the table. That was all."

Cela planted red geraniums, paperwhites and begonias in the boxes at the window ledges. "The people looked forward to our coming," she says. "It became a gala event the few days we were there."

In a report, Fred Sloman wrote that "at the Antice stop children, mothers and fathers almost hugged and kissed our school. The hard part was to give them but four days." He remarked that "there was no satisfying their appetite for knowledge."

Betty Dingee Etier, who lived on Ground Hog River, remembers traveling to Kukatush, the next-to-last car stop on Fred Sloman's line. Aged seven, eight and nine, the three Dingee children traveled on skis, snowshoes and dogsled. They covered the seven miles to Kukatush on an eight-foot toboggan pulled by five dogs. "We picked up Indian children along

This frightened little girl came to school on a speeder—a one man hand pumped car. It was similar to a handcar that needed four men to operate. The little girl, who spoke no English, had arrived from Italy only the night before. - CN Archives

15

Six-year-old Donna Jean Smith arrives at the school car on the Kukatush siding. Her father was keeper of the dam on Ground Hog River.

the way," she says. "And when we crossed the frozen lake, we marked the trail every thirty feet with an evergreen branch, just in case the wind blew over the path during the day." They tied the dogs to a tree. After an all-day wait, the dogs sped the children home at 4 p.m. when school ended. In warmer weather the Dingee children paddled their canoe four miles down Ground Hog River, then they walked two miles along the track to Kukatush.

Molly Legault, a student on a Canadian Pacific rail car, came from a family of twelve children. She remembers the life of her family centered around the coming of the school car. "We had to get our homework done," she says. "We had to get in so much wood and water. We had to get everyone's clothes ready. It was as if we were getting ready for Christmas or Easter." Molly welcomed the school car's coming, for it gave relief from the dishes and all the housework in a fourteen-member family.

Cela Sloman describes her husband as a big, tall man who showed great patience. "He never was cross. Things just moved at an even keel with him," she says. He never went into the schoolroom unless he wore a tie and blue shirt. "He was always neat and tidy," she says.

He rolled back the long sleeves of his shirt so no cuffs showed at his wrists under his coat jacket. "And often he wore in the schoolroom old galoshes," she says, "because he might have to get off suddenly and hand something to a passing train."

Fred Sloman kept each school day brimmed with activity. He taught new lessons and reviewed old ones. He worked individually with the students. He checked homework and gave out new assignments. "Every night we had at least an hour and a half of homework," recalls one student. And Mr. Sloman kept the students in plenty of homework during his month-long absence.

In the school car the children learned and recited multiplication tables. They looked up new words in the dictionary. They labeled towns on the map. They read a history lesson and drew a watercolour to illustrate it. They listed their birthdays each month on the calendar. They memorized rules of grammar. They learned by heart long passages of poems.

Fred Sloman rings the school bell.

Northern school bus?

Fred Sloman instructs his students.

Fred Sloman stands at the head of the class. Cela tends to her plants and the dogs look out of the window.

19

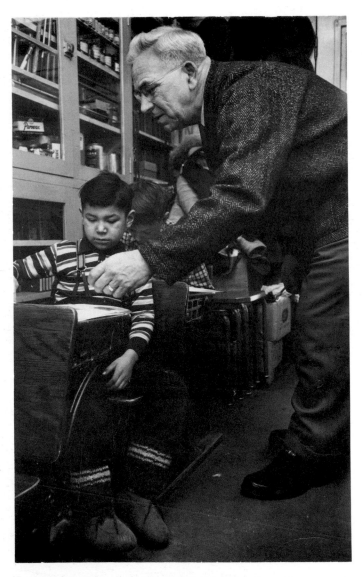

Fred Sloman looks over the work of student Clifford Beaucage, aged 6, at Thor Lake.

Once they drew a train on a sixteen-foot-long adding machine paper. They made a fire tower in a toy village and learned about fire safety. Mr. Sloman held carpentry classes outside. His students used hammers and saws and made useful items for home and school.

Cela Sloman remembers that once her husband satisfied a few older boys who felt uncomfortable in a class of youngsters. "He told them they were Special B," she says. "Then they didn't feel so bad."

Fred Sloman took great pride in the accomplishments of his students. He once wrote:

> "If we find a child who knows a and b and c, we teach him d. If he happens to be one who can do simple equations in algebra, we teach him simultaneous equations, and if it is a pupil who knows about Vienna and Naples, we teach him about Calgary and Montreal."

Mrs. Sloman says that two types of students came to the school car. The one group belonged to the families of the local railroad section men, trappers and hunters. The second came from Sudbury during the Depression years, where they lived in abandoned shacks in the surrounding bush country. There the families hunted and found enough wood to survive. These children knew city life and had attended schools. "They were harder to control," says Cela.

By contrast the native bush children were shy and reserved. They entered the strange and frightening world of the classroom. Betty

Students play with the toy farm at the Anstice stop. "They had little acquaintance with barnyard and farm animals," says Cela.

A student named David. - CN Archives

Two students look at a map with teacher Fred Sloman at the Anstice stop. - CN Archives

Eight year old Mike Evanush who walked three miles to school from Ground Hog River.

- CN Archives

Etier remembers how the Sloman children helped them to adapt to their new surroundings. They talked and made friends with the quiet children of the bush.

Discipline wasn't a persistent problem on the school cars however. Helen Wright, wife of school car teacher William Wright, says, "The students respected the teacher. They came to school as if it were a church." In the thirty-nine years her husband taught in the Canadian Pacific car, on two different routes, no scratch was ever carved into the desks. "There was no leapfrogging over desks either," she says. "The students took off their boots at the back of the school, and they came to their desks in stocking feet."

During the war years Fred Sloman encouraged his students to save their pennies to buy stamps for war certificates. At the time, Betty Dingee Etier was fourteen years old. She and her sister cut thirty-six cords of hardwood with a crosscut saw and bought war stamps. They earned more money by chopping a cord of wood for twenty-five cents. On the blackboard at the front of the classroom Mr. Sloman posted the amount of money the children donated for the war effort.

Betty Etier recalls that Fred Sloman not only knew his subject matter, but he also excelled in keeping his students' attention. She never forgot the little wooden dog hut that hung up behind Mr. Sloman's desk. Whenever he felt he was losing the students' attention, he started to pull the dog out of the hut. Its body grew longer and longer. "And you'd start staring at Mr. Sloman," laughs Betty. "But you'd be watching this dog coming out. But the other end of the dog never did come out!" With his collapsible wooden dog, Fred Sloman had the students back on track.

Betty Etier says Mr. Sloman collected many artifacts from the North. The children once gave him a rabbit skeleton. He wired it so the skeleton came down on a string. He had the Indians make snowshoes for him, and he used them as visual aids for a lesson.

Bill Sloman explains to a younger child the home made "time machine".   - CN Archives

The students build a toy railroad out of tie plugs in a crowded classroom. These small pieces of wood were used under the tie plates that supported the rails.

CN Archives

Fred Sloman and child.

He also charmed the students with his story about the fairy named Dub, who lived on top of the blackboard. He told the students the fairy was too shy to come out, but that the fairy sent down candies and sweets to him for the children.

Fred Sloman wove fanciful stories about his fairy. He carried on conversations with her and the students overheard them. One of his best-loved stories about the fairy revealed her origins. "Don't you know," he asked, "that when the first child was born on earth and smiled, the Creator liked the smile so much that he turned it into a fairy or a guardian angel?" He said that ever since that time, when a baby gives its first smile, it immediately has a fairy. "And every fairy has a name and mine is so beautiful," he went on, "that I was afraid someone else would take her, so I changed her name to Dub ... You see, during your childhood your smiles are lovely to behold, and therefore so is your fairy. But when you grow up, your smiles change to smirks and each one hurts your fairy, eventually crippling her."

Mr. Sloman explained that now, since his own Dub was growing older, she was becoming cranky. She even had a broken wing. But she kept enough of her early good nature and continued to send down the candies for the children.

The school car had its own small museum. And in a box, about two feet wide and one and a half feet high, stood a miniature church.

Fredda Sloman cuts a slip from a plant.

Fred Sloman's desk and wall shelves. The bamboo hoop was used to put off messages. As the train passed and slowed down, the hoop was grabbed from the engineer or conductor.

It had an altar, cross, baptismal font, organ, pews, stained-glass window, reredos and a bishop's chair. Above the homemade church were nailed small rectangles crafted out of scrap iron. With a hammer and nail, the students pounded into the metal the names of outstanding religious figures. "I don't know whether General Booth, Martin Luther and Archbishop Thomas Cranmer would appreciate being placed side by side," said Fred Sloman, "but it's the best we can do here."

Fred Sloman was the first to admit that he presided over a cluttered classroom. He once said, "The school room isn't a tidy place — too much junk. We have to display the bit of lace that somebody made, the axe handle carved with designs, the photographs of someone's hometown in Europe and the hundred cans of things that the pickle company gave us for bingo prizes."

His own desk and the bookshelving on the wall next to it presented a nightmare's maze, but he knew where everything was. "If anyone asked him for something, he reached his hand up and pulled it down," says Cela.

Daughter Margaret Sloman remembers that her father believed in frequent recesses. "'Airing out' he called them." Her father sent them out to play even when it was 45° F below zero. Garlic, wet mocassins and goose grease rubbed on a child's chest as protection against colds created their own exotic aromas. Often underwear stayed on all winter. There was no running water for baths and washing, since the rivers were frozen.

Airing Out time.

The school car on a siding.

"Kids and their fathers and mothers in the bush had been taught that linoleum on a floor and 30-cent curtains on the windows were the perquisites of the rich. Father Time had told them they were poor instead of being told they were valuable."

Fred Sloman

Before the arrival of the school car, hundreds of children in the bush country went without any formal education. Their families lived over vast distances and in remote areas. They often kept on the move. Roads were few. The waterways — lakes, rivers and streams — were the main routes of transportation.

When the railroad cut its tracks through the northern wilderness of rock, river, lake and bush, many immigrants came to work on the lines. Every seven miles of railroad track made up a section. A foreman and several other workmen maintained it. Italian immigrants often worked as section men. "They were the only ones who would stay through the flies of summer and the cold of winter," says Cela Sloman. "They were frugal and anxious to get ahead."

The men often returned to Italy and brought back their brides. They raised their large families near the tracks in small clusters of little shanties. Since the section men left home early in the morning to work on the tracks, their wives and children were left alone all day. They had few or no neighbours at all. And even if they happened to see their neighbours from miles away, they probably couldn't understand them, for they spoke different languages. This new way of life in Canada overwhelmed the young Italian women, who were used to living with relatives and friends nearby. In the small Italian villages they often worked together communally.

For the children of the North the Department of Education offered a few programs, such as correspondence courses, traveling libraries, consolidated schools, and a boarding school in Monteith. But these proved useless to the majority of families who spoke no English. The close-knit families would never dream of sending away their children to a school for days and weeks at a time. The building of local one-room schoolhouses, like those that flourished in the southern part of the province, was impractical. Geography, funding and sparcity of population weighed against it.

The plight of these children in the North had burdened Fred Sloman. At the beginning of their marriage, Fred and Cela spent two bitterly cold winters in Krugerdorf, a small community on the Temiskaming and Northern Ontario Railroad. There Fred taught school and cut his own wood for both the schoolhouse and their own home.

Fred expressed his concerns in a letter to J. B. MacDougall, the school inspector at North

Canadian Pacific School Car, 1925

- Canadian Pacific Corporate Archives

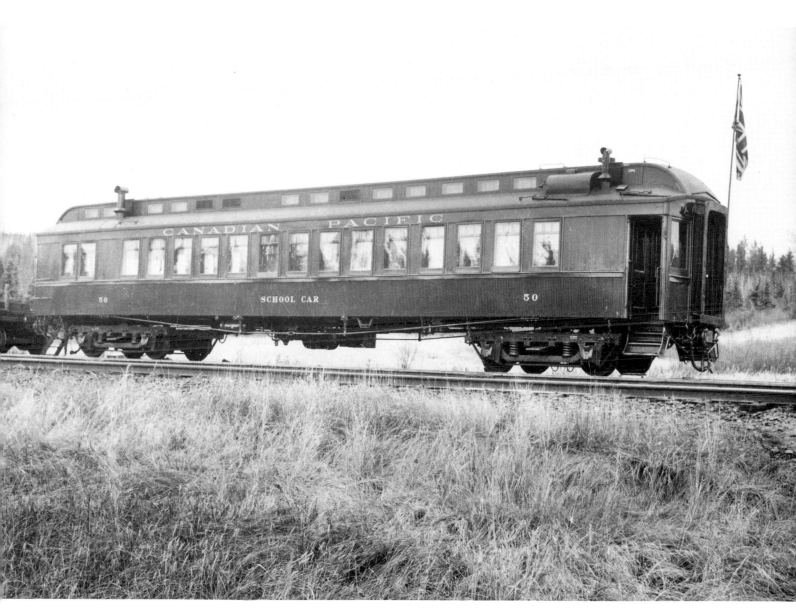

Canadian Pacific School Car.

- Canadian Pacific Corporate Archives

Bay and principal of the Normal School there. Mr. Sloman offered to put a pack on his back and travel through the bush country on skis and snowshoes and teach children wherever he found them.

The school inspector was equally troubled over the lack of education in the North. As early as 1922 he pleaded for improved services. He felt some policy and "added devices," as he called them, were necessary. In his education report of that year he suggested the possibility of a traveling school or an itinerant teacher. He felt that if children could not be brought to education, then education should be brought to them.

The idea of using the railroad had begun to take shape in his mind. One day he saw a switching train push some railroad service cars onto a spur track. The thought struck him. The very track that shackled families to the rails could also free them. Why not have a railcar travel the tracks?

The plan was not unlike the circuit of the old Methodist "connexion." Instead of an itinerant saddlebag preacher who covered a prescribed route on horseback over and over again, a teacher would go from siding to siding. He would stay from three to six days and then move on. In about a month he would return and repeat his route once again.

For many people the scheme sounded too bold and extravagant. But J. B. MacDougall won the support of the Premier of Ontario, G. Howard Ferguson, who also served at the same time as Minister of Education. Inspector MacDougall also found the two railroads willing to join in the venture.

Canadian National and Canadian Pacific and the Department of Education struck an agreement. The Department would supply the teachers, teaching materials and fixtures, such as books, desks, blackboards, maps, microscopes, notebooks, pencils and a small library. It would also work out the itinerary. The railroads agreed to supply the cars and, at government expense, convert the cars into a combination schoolroom and living quarters. The freight trains would move the school car to its siding. And the railway would maintain and service the cars.

What began as a six-month venture resulted in a forty-one-year education program for the children of the isolated North. The Department of Education preferred the use of the term "car school." The railroads more commonly used the term "school car." Yet Fred Sloman attests to the fact that very early his car was named "School-On-Wheels" —painted on in gold letters against the olive green of the CN car's wooden siding.

In 1928 two more railcars were converted to schools. The Canadian National contributed one car, the Canadian Pacific the other. These cars served out of the present-day city of Thunder Bay, then known as the twin cities of Port Arthur and Fort William. The Canadian Pacific train headed out of Fort

William through Ignace to Kenora. The CNR car traveled north from Port Arthur to Sioux Lookout. In 1930 CN added a third car that traveled west out of Port Arthur to Fort Frances.

With all of the school cars, the itinerary altered as the number of students rose, fell or completely disappeared. The population might fluctuate from year to year, or from season to season. This flexibility of schedule was the genius of the school car system. The minimum number of students needed for a stop at a siding was set at four.

In 1934 the Canadian National added another car, bringing its total to four school cars. It originally ran from Sioux Lookout to the Manitoba border. The Temiskaming and Northern Ontario Railroad, now the Ontario Northland, added a seventh car in 1938. This car served the Laurentian region of northeastern Ontario.

The school car system reached its peak in the 1940s. It served an area of over a thousand miles. Four cars traveled the Canadian National tracks, two rode on the Canadian Pacific lines and one on the Temiskaming and Northern Ontario Railroad. The cars served 226 students.

Elizabeth Sloman raises the flag as another school day begins.

Two students play spin-the-top.

"A thousand curses on the man who invented the monotonous game of bingo — and a thousand blessings. In cities you can entertain your guests in more adult fashion. But if your guests range from four to over seventy, some game must be found that all can play."

Fred Sloman

School car teachers never ended their day at four in the afternoon. "We had trouble getting the students to go home," recalls Cela Sloman. But the Slomans needed a few hours in the late afternoon for supper and for the preparation of the evening activities.

Section men, unable to read and write, came to the school car at night for instruction. "In one week they were able to write their names," says Cela. "They gripped their pens so hard, the blood ran out of their hands."

Mrs. Sloman helped the women by writing letters and sending orders to Eatons and Simpsons. She taught sewing and dressmaking. She talked to them about hygiene and child care. The Slomans became explainers and interpreters of the Canadian way of life. They told the immigrants about the parliamentary system and democratic ideals.

Pasquale Deciccio, a school car student, recalls that during the Second World War the Royal Canadian Mounted Police made regular checks on the Italian community. His father was among them. Fred Sloman tried to explain to him the reason for this wartime measure.

When the school car idea had begun to take shape, the Premier hoped the school would teach more than the basic skills of English reading, writing and arithmetic. He believed it could introduce the immigrants to the Canadian way of life, instil democratic principles, and foster national loyalty and good citizenship.

The school car lent as many as a thousand books each school term. Sloman reported that the borrowers were scrupulously honest in returning them. And when he talked to them about the content, their response revealed they had read and understood the books.

The community along the rails looked to the school car for social activity and recreation. Fred Sloman fixed the desks so they would slide back. The school could then hold as many as sixty people. They loved to play bingo and crokinole. Fred organized teams of crokinole players at the various mileage points. The winners competed in tournaments at Capreol. The Slomans awarded prizes, such as chocolate bars and other small gifts, to the winners. The women especially treasured the prizes of baby powder, new bottles and nipples. "They never had those things in the Far North," says Cela.

In 1930 Fred Sloman bought a movie projector, whose light was powered by a battery from his Model A Ford car. He turned the film through by hand and then rewound it the same way. He borrowed films wherever he could find someone to lend them to him. Through these home pictures he introduced the Northern people to such commonplace items as verandas, bicycles, water taps and garden hoses. He later secured commercial films to show as well.

With his own movie camera he took pictures of his pupils and their families. And when they saw themselves on the screen, they marveled. Mr. Sloman undertook another movie film project, one that brought tears of joy to his people. He arranged for Kodak representatives who were traveling in Italy one summer to take a few rolls of film in designated towns, streets and homes. He asked for close-ups. Months later Mr. Sloman showed the familiar scenes and faces to the immigrants who had left years before. They treasured the films, shown over and over again until they almost wore out.

In wintertime the nearby frozen rivers became skating rinks. Sometimes the Slomans brought a gramophone down to the river and they all skated to the music. Cela Sloman recalls that wolves howled in the background.

"It was a week of sports as well as school," says Mary Frazer, whose husband Philip taught on a Canadian National school car. They brought along in their car skates, toboggans and skis provided by auxiliary groups across the province in the Canadian South. These women's auxiliaries, along with the Imperial Order of the Daughters of the Empire, provided clothing, toys and household utensils. The daughter of Dr. J. B.

MacDougall was instrumental in organizing these womens' auxiliaries.

The school car teachers received their own special gifts. In their eagerness to say "thank you" to the teachers, the parents gave what they had — a chicken or a rabbit, vegetables, home-baked goods and fresh cream.

In a magazine article, Fred Sloman wrote about the prized gift he received from an immigrant lad who walked five miles through the snow several evenings a week to the school car. This young man came after he finished work in the lumber camps at 7 p.m. and then walked back at midnight. But once, two days before Christmas, the lad arrived at the school car in the afternoon, when Fred Sloman was teaching sixteen small children, who were busy at their lessons. Mr. Sloman, who delighted in telling stories, described the incident: "Perhaps in his land the kindliest gift you can bring is one of wine and a chicken that is still alive. And as the young man walked down the aisle he took the newspaper wrapping off a parcel and planted a bottle of whiskey on my desk. It was a big bottle — the forty-ounce size that they sell in Montreal.

"The Minister of Education gives us a handbook covering rules and regulations. Search as I could in the index, I could find no paragraph covering the disciplinary measures that should be taken when a student leaves a bottle of whiskey on the teacher's desk while school is in session. There was nothing to do but keep the bottle until someone issued a rule to cover the situation."

A group of women who came to visit the school car. Some visitors arrived unexpectedly. If the transcontinental train—the Flyer—had a stopover or delay near the school car siding, the passengers might go through on a tour.

At Kukatush Bill Sloman tried his hand at "skinning the cat". He flips himself over the clothes line prop his mother used to raise her laundry higher off the ground.   - CN Archives

"I just taught the A B C and the two plus two ... and hoped to instill a dream, but there is no metre to measure such intangibles as the conception of a dream."

Fred Sloman

Until the school car came into the North, its children lived in a world circumscribed by bush. Education expanded their horizons. It opened a window on the world. It changed their lives.

A number received scholastic recognition. Mr. Sloman once was asked to relate the greatest success story of one of his students. He replied in a letter,

"I would not dare answer this. Conscience forbids it. It's the same when ... I have to give a prize for the 'best' speller or the 'best' Latin grammar student ... On the ladder we are supposed to travel between heaven and earth, it just happens that he who makes the first or third rung only, has done a greater thing than he who steps from rung sixty-nine to rung three score ten and the heavenly lights.

"I am a man with a hoe, eyes naturally down to the mud instead of to the stars. The one single prize reward I won away beyond all other prizes and rewards was when a fourteen year old lad came to school for Grade 1 and stayed until he was fourteen and a half. Saying goodbye, he lingered and looking from a window at the rain said, 'Jez, it's good to get education. Used to be if you had to do something like, say, go back to the lake for the cow, or cut some wood, it took hours and hours to do it. Now if you do some rotten job like that, you get to thinking of what makes the clouds or looking at a bug, or seeing how rocks are in layers and just things like that. The first thing you know it's time to quit work and you don't know you're tired or fed up.'"

Fred Sloman took dramatic steps to make sure his students not only heard about the wider world, but actually saw it. He took them to Capreol and Sudbury. And when his bank account climbed over $100, he felt he could afford to take some of his students to Toronto for a trip. City officials arranged a tour of the city that included Casa Loma, luncheon at the Granite Club and the top of skyscrapers.

On one trip the mayor of Toronto asked the students if they wanted to see anything special. One boy spoke up and said he'd like to see where the city threw away all of its old tin cans. Keeping his promise, the mayor sent the boy out to the dump in his own private car.

At other times Fred Sloman took students to larger cities when he spoke to organizations about his work in the North. Through these speaking engagements he secured the support of these groups and he introduced the students to streetcars, sidewalks and Ferris wheels at fairgrounds.

These trips made indelible impressions on the students. Years later one former student gave Fred Sloman $50. He said, "Use it to give another kid the break you gave me."

Humorous stories reveal how unfamiliar the students were with the outside world. Molly Legault tells about the time when her little brother took part in a recital on the school car. After her brother finished his performance, the teacher told him to bow. The little fellow had never heard of such a thing. "The only bow he knew was bow-wow," laughs Molly, "and that's what he did. He said 'Bow-wow.'"

Another school car teacher, Andrew Clement, recalls that some Indian children didn't know how to use a desk. They walked into the schoolroom and sat down on top of the desks. They thought the seat was the place where they placed their feet.

Fred Sloman wrote a story for a newspaper about one unusual day of teaching. A father, mother, sister-in-law and six children arrived unannounced at the school car. "The father's face was beaming with pride and the kids' faces were polished like bronze," wrote Fred Sloman. "And the father said, 'My children come for their education.'"

Fred made room for six more children in his already crowded classroom. And all day long the father, mother and sister-in-law squatted in one position hour after hour at the end of the school car. "They focused their hawk-like gazes on me every minute," wrote Fred.

He started to wonder if the family planned to stay for the night. But when Fred closed his book and the other students packed up their lessons to take home, the Indian family stood up and prepared to leave. From their disjointed remarks he realized they didn't intend to return. Fred reported, "The father said, 'Now my children have been educated.' They had crowded a lifetime of knowledge into a day. And they stole away. I've never seen them since."

Molly Legault tells another story about one of her brothers. She knows it was often said that people cried when the school car left the siding for its next stop. Tears came to their eyes as the car pulled away. Molly admits that her brother cried alright. But he cried when he saw the school car coming. He didn't have his homework started!

The school car story found its way into many Canadian newspapers and magazines. It appeared in *Life* magazine, the *New York Times, London Times* and the *Reader's Digest.*

Royalty came to visit the school car. Only several months after the Slomans started their run, Prince George paid them a visit. In 1939, as King George, he and his wife Queen Elizabeth visited them. Lady Baden-Powell lingered over an hour in the Sloman school car, even though her schedule had allotted only a ten-minute stay. In their guest book

The students decorate the car for the visit of King George V in July 1939.

the Slomans have signatures of Dr. V. K. Greer, Gordon Sinclair, Agnes MacPhail, Donald Gordon and Dr. Frederick Banting.

Fred Sloman contributed many vignettes and stories to the newspapers about his life on the school car. He also wrote short stories, several of which won literary awards. One of his most poignant stories describes the day in July 1939 when the King's train passed along the section of track maintained by an immigrant named Pete.

"You might see him any day patroling the fourteen miles of track and carrying a heavy hammer, claw-bar and shovel," wrote Fred Sloman. "His job is the kind that makes a man grow old before his time. Not only the dull heavy pick and claw-bar do that, but there is the loneliness. And there are bears and if it is winter there may be wolves that make a noise that sickens the heart if you are fourteen miles away alone."

Pete lived in a bunkhouse without his

family, who had remained in Italy. His wife, suffering from a lung disease, was not allowed to enter the country. Pete had never seen his youngest daughter, Therese.

The foreman had told Pete to walk the fourteen-mile section that day and to check with care all the bolts and anglebars and switches. And then he was to stand at Mile 132.6, on the small overhead bridge above the tracks, and wait until the King's train passed.

"He waited there two hours and nineteen minutes," reported Fred Sloman. "It was hot. The sun in these parts comes back from the rocks as from a stove. The flies are worse this year than we have ever known them before. There were strict orders that nobody was to light a fire near the track on the day their King was to pass through. That is why Pete did not make a smoke smudge against the flies. They made a ring of bites that bled where his hat met his forehead. When he brushed them from the back of his neck his hand came away with blood on it.

"Then the King's train passed. Pete stood up. He didn't know if you were allowed to look or not. But he did look, sort of sideways ... For as a train passes, a trackman is supposed to look at the wheels to see if maybe a brake beam or a rod is dragging. And then when it has passed, you are supposed to step quickly to the track and work hard with a pick or a claw-bar, for there might be a boss on the tail of that train. Bosses expect to see men working and not staring at the train.

"Pete did just that. He did not see if there was a boss or a King or a Queen. He dug his shovel into the stones until the train went around the curve.

"Then he looked up — and there not two rail lengths from him were the roses! They were lying on the sun hot stones and they were not much crushed ...

"I would not believe the Queen had given flowers to Pete if I hadn't seen them with my own eyes. I saw them on his bunkhouse table. He put them in a jug and spread a white handkerchief from his trunk for them.

"There are twenty-seven of them and three are broken. They are woven in and out with a sort of net stuff that feels like silk and they have a pretty smell to them yet. The roses seem to shine like a light. They make the smoke-stained walls of the bunkhouse, the trusted stove and granite plate and the cup that Pete uses to make his supper look different.

"Tomorrow we are going to pack them in a carton with moss from the rocks. And when a train stops at the watertank we will ask a trainman to post them when he gets to town.

"They are for Therese. She is nearly nine years old now.

"Of course the roses will be dead as dry dust long before they are half way across the sea. But they are a gift from a Queen."

"Dr. J. B. MacDougall didn't know anyone else foolish enough to take on the job, so he gave it to me."

Fred Sloman

The school car required extraordinary teachers. They not only had to possess the skills to teach in an ungraded classroom, but they had to know how to endure the rigours of a long six-month winter. They had to be hardy, resourceful and self-reliant. They also needed to establish sympathetic and warm contact with immigrant families. They had to get along with the railway workers.

They gave up year-round companionship of close friends, neighbours and other teachers. They waved at many people who sped past on trains, but they never shook their hands. Regular church attendance was impossible. They lived without supermarkets and the other facilities and amenities of life in Southern Ontario.

"The work grows on you," says school car teacher Angus McKay, "for you catch the dedication and belief of the late Dr. J. B. MacDougall. He felt the school cars couldn't do anything wrong. You couldn't let him down. You wouldn't dare."

When Angus McKay left the school car to join the army during World War II, his wife Helen took over his work. She was the only woman who officially taught on the school cars. The McKays served on two different lines from 1934 to 1946.

When school car teacher Cameron Bell died in 1949, his wife Florence took over his teaching post for two years, but unofficially.

School car teachers knew how to adapt. They often stayed on longer if they were married. Their wives not only helped out with an occasional lesson or taught the children English, but they joined in the recreation and social life on the school cars. Their presence and help broke an otherwise isolated existence.

Fred and Cela Sloman drink coffee in their living quarters.
- Robert C. Ragsdale

45

Helen and Bill Wright, 1956.

Helen Wright feels she and her husband had a better marriage because of their years on the school car. "When you live together twenty-four hours a day," she says, "you have to get along. There's no other way. You grew to understand one another better. There were no distractions."

Philip Fraser taught on the school car three years before he married. "He said he wasn't going to stay there alone any longer," recalls Mary Fraser, "if I didn't come and keep house for him." Philip suggested that they marry in the spring so they could live a few months in the North on the car and see if she liked it. "And if I didn't, then he would plan to change locations," says Mrs. Fraser, "but I loved the North." She laughs and says she knew what she was in for.

Fred Sloman learned to live with the noise and vibration of the "Flyer," the transcontinental train that sped by on the main line only nine feet from the school car siding. Betty Etier recalls the few times the easy-going Fred Sloman became perturbed. "It would get him a little mad when a big freight would go by," she says. "He'd be into a lecture and this steam engine would get blowing at him, sort of saying 'Hello,' but he couldn't hear a thing."

Keeping the water circulating in the car's heating system in the winter required the teacher's constant attention. The cars had never been designed to be heated for months on end by stoves. Every teacher was warned against letting the pipes freeze. A major freeze-up would require the car to go back into the shop for repair.

Any damage to the pipes was costly enough, but even greater damage came to the teacher's reputation. One school car teacher from England failed to stoke the coal stove just right, his train burned up, and that ended not only the car's run, but the teacher's career on the school car as well.

A Baker heating system was the standard heating unit in a railroad coach. It was like an upright cylinder with a heating coil inside. This furnace, as the Slomans called it, was fueled by coal and it stood in the kitchen. The hot water circulated down one side of the car, crossed over and came back the other side into the furnace. "It was a complicated set-up," says school car teacher William Wright, "but all you had to do was keep a good fire going. You'd hear the water rolling through every few minutes. That was music to your ears. If you woke up and heard that sound at night, you went right back to sleep again."

Student Betty Etier remembers the times Fred Sloman crawled underneath the school car and tried to thaw his water lines. Daughter Margaret Sloman says, "My father taught school all day and then he had to worry about the circulation of the water at night. It made such a friendly sound—click, click, click, click, click."

Below-zero temperatures required constant vigil from her father. He might climb out of bed four and five times a night to check on the pipes. Fred Sloman's subconscious mind worked overtime even in the summer. He'd wake up with a start and reach over to feel if the steam pipes were frozen.

The school car's living quarters were cramped. The Sloman's first car, an old fifty-two- foot wooden truss-rod passenger coach, was built in 1898 at the Hochelaga Shops in Montreal. The Canadian National used it as an office car when it constructed new rail lines in 1908.

The car was divided about equally between schoolroom and living quarters. The school measured twenty-two feet long. The remainder of the car consisted of bathroom, combination bedroom-living room and kitchen. Heater and storage space took up four and a half feet at the one end. This meagre amount of room proved especially inadequate for the growing Sloman family.

For several years the Slomans were promised a larger and more substantial car. In 1938 the railway shop of Temiskaming and Northern Ontario Railroad at North Bay refurbished a second-class coach into a sixty-eight-foot-long school car under Fred Sloman's direction. But on its way to Capreol, the car caught fire. It was completely gutted.

The Slomans waited until 1940 before they received their newly outfitted car. Once again Fred Sloman directed the rebuilding of the car, a CNR eighty-foot-long railcar at the London, Ontario, shops. Built in 1914, the car now became the School-On-Wheels #15089. The chief inspector reported that the school car was "the last word in workmanship, comfort and convenience." A newspaper account described the kitchen as a "city wife's dream, made of stainless steel metal. Its bathroom is enamel. Its living room is buff and cream with built-in bunks and cupboards and diaper dryers."

For many years the Slomans believed their new school car had once been a dining car, built in 1914. But in 1986 Gerald Buck, a member of the Canadian Railroad Historical Association, brought forward new information. He verified that 1914 was the date of the car's building. He named the Crossen Car and Manufacturing Company of Cobourg, Ontario, as its builder. He says this series of car was one of the last manufactured by the Crossens, for the company went out of railcar building the next year.

He identified the car as a colonist car, not a dining car. It was built for the Canadian Northern Railways, a predecessor railroad of the Canadian National. Its original number was C Nor #1249 Colonist Car. When it became part of the Canadian National Railways, the car was called C. N. #2648 Colonist Car.

Gerald Buck's uncle, Fred Buck, probably helped to convert the car in the London Yards in 1940. Gerald Buck's father, Frank, was a carman in Toronto who worked on the car many times in the yards after it was retired from service.

Gerald Buck describes a colonist car as a second-class car that provided a less costly way for immigrants and other travelers to get out West. "It was a barebones car," he says. Its seats folded down so the passengers could sleep on their way across the country. It had its own stove for cooking and a long table for meals.

"We teach in the front and live at the back — even have a bathtub that can be filled with water carried from a lake. In the livingspace of 46 feet by 9 my wife, Cela, has raised five children, and they all have stayed until they reached Grade 13 of high school."

Fred Sloman

In the new school car the teaching area now measured twenty-six feet by nine feet. But the Slomans continued to use coal oil for their lamps and coal for their Baker furnace that stood in the kitchen. They fed wood into the Quebec heater in the schoolroom. "It consumed cord after cord of wood from the boxes placed strategically along the miles of track," reported Fred Sloman. Their school car never had electricity.

The kitchen held the monster of a cookstove, removed from their first school car. "I wanted that big, ugly stove," says Cela. "You couldn't clean it too well, but it made good bread."

She continued to wash the family clothes on a scrub board in a metal washtub. "There

The commodious Sloman living room.

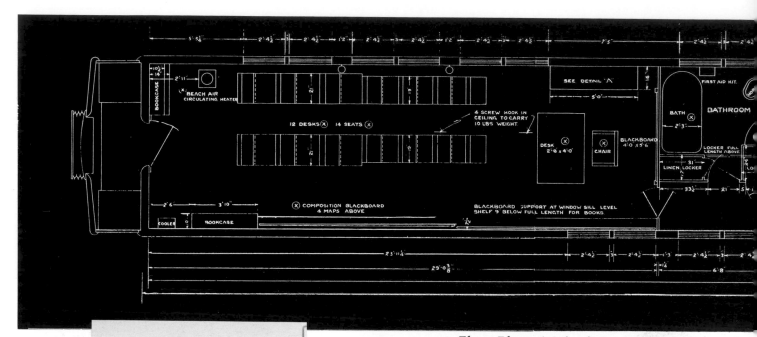

Floor Plan of School Car #15089 from the

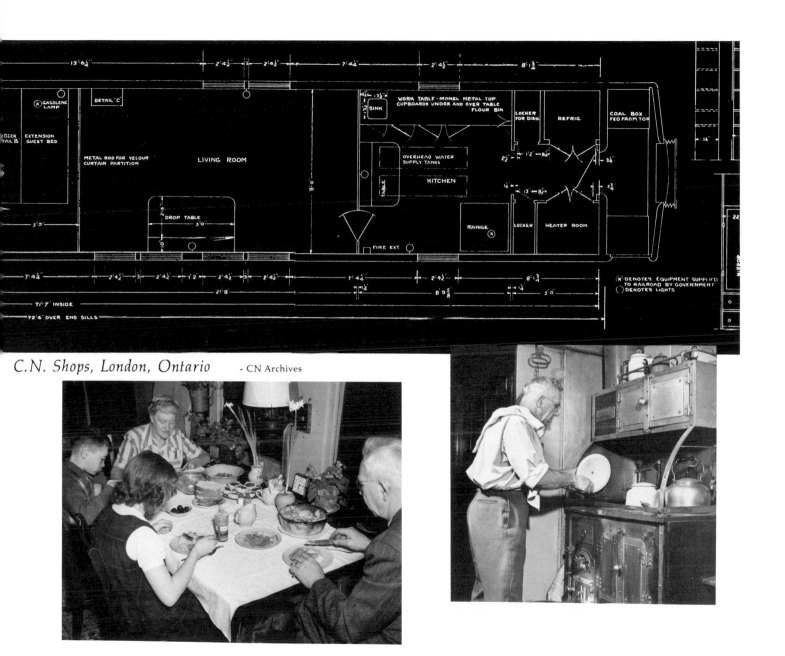

C.N. Shops, London, Ontario   - CN Archives

was no other way," she says. "You got water from the rivers and heated it on the kitchen stove." She hung out her laundry to dry on a clothesline stretched between posts, telegraph poles or trees. She also did her own dry cleaning in a washtub.

Cela learned to live with railroad soot and the smell of grease, coal and steam. She sewed clothes for the family. The last two of their children were twins, Fredda and William, born in 1938. The older children included Joan, Elizabeth and Margaret.

Cela's help extended beyond the school car and her own family. "Once I went back into the bush a half a mile to visit a sick baby," she recalls. "The mother was alone with her children. Her husband was working in a bush camp. The older children, who attended school, told the Slomans their mother needed help. After Cela tended the sick newborn, she started on her way back home. A dog came up and followed along at her side. "He escorted me home," she says. When she told Fred about the dog, he looked outside the window and saw the animal. "That's no dog," he said. "That's a wolf." Every local dog was known and recognized at every mileage point. "If I had known that," she told Fred, "I wouldn't have patted him on the head."

Animals, including that friendly wolf, were all part of Sloman family life in the North. "We always had a cat," says Cela. "That's besides the two dogs named Sandy and Cricket. And we had a crow, and once a fox that was getting his leg repaired. And of course Petunia, the skunk." Cela quickly adds that Petunia was deskunked before they took her up to the school car. Their young son William found the baby skunk in Clinton, where the Slomans stayed at Fred's family home every summer. "The mother and all the babies were killed going across the street, except this one," she says. "He brought it home all wrapped up in his shirt."

Petunia stayed in the school car with the Slomans all that winter. "She was a beautiful skunk," says Cela. "Everyone knew her. And she got awfully smart too. She'd get out of her box at night, lie on her back and kick at the swinging door between the kitchen and living room. She'd get the door to swinging, then right herself and walk into the living room." One night Mrs. Sloman wakened and put her foot down at the end of the bed. "I felt something furry," she says. "It was Petunia."

When spring came, Petunia wanted to be out in the wilds on her own. The Slomans took her across on an island and left her there.

For the school car families Christmas extended over a whole month, for at each stop they celebrated the season with Christmas carols, concerts and parties. They brought in a cedar from the bush and decorated the car and tree in ornaments and tinsel. On the outside of the Sloman car, the students hung up letters that spelled out "Merry Christmas." The Slomans embraced the children of the North and their parents as

The students put up the Christmas tree taken from the bush. The dogs lend their help.

an extended family. One Christmas Eve their school car was towed to Capreol, for it needed its frozen pipes thawed. The entire Sloman family spent Christmas Day singing carols with the roundhouse men.

Whenever the Slomans needed occasional repairs to their car or its pipes thawed, the school car was pulled right inside the shops. The Slomans continued to live in it. "And when the workmen left at night," she says, "they gave us the keys to the shop."

Their monthly return to Capreol allowed the family to shop, go on errands and visit the barbershop. They attended worship services at whatever church was open that Sunday. In Capreol they stored their Model A Ford for the winter, after returning from summer holidays in Clinton.

In the *Weekend Magazine* in 1954 Fred Sloman wrote, "Unfortunately I like this life of teaching in the bush, like an alcoholic likes strong drink. It is a misfortune, for I still drive a Model 'A' car and have to content myself with dreaming of the day I shall travel to Montreal and Victoria and see neon lights and flower pots that hang on lamp posts."

In the Depression years hobos often came to the school car. Mrs. Sloman couldn't turn them away. She sometimes baked twice a day. She fed them freshly baked bread with brown sugar sprinkled on top.

Margaret Sloman remembers the fright of her life. The night was bitterly cold. Her mother and father finished drinking their coffee in the schoolroom. She took their cups out into the kitchen to fill them up again. She rushed back to her parents and exclaimed, "There's a man in the oven!"

Fred Sloman said the man must be cold. They thawed him out with hot soup and coffee. Cela held the dish to his mouth, for his hands were shaking. He drank cup after cup. He stayed over for the night and left the next morning. The man never talked. He only nodded. "We wondered how cold he was the next night," says Margaret. "It was 60° below."

During these Depression years, when many transients passed through, the Canadian National ordered the Slomans to pull their blinds at night to lessen the risk of break-ins and other disturbances. But the Slomans would not close off the light, for the school car was the only light on the bleak siding. "Let there be light," said Fred Sloman.

Ever since the Slomans heard about a woman who sat up all night to watch their lights, they wanted to keep as many lamps burning as possible. The two gasoline lamps that hung from the school car's ceiling sent out much brighter light than the coal oil in brackets along the side of the car. The Slomans felt that more than one woman used to sit and gaze at their lights until the grey dawn streaked the skies.

Once a baby was born on the Sloman school car. Fred Sloman wrote, "I dismissed the school to have the school car ready for a freight train to come and take us to town where there would be a doctor." But the train

Mothers arrive to help decorate Christmas boxes.

came late. "I christened the baby before it died," he wrote. "And for that the mother thanked me. Maybe it mattered."

"A teacher never knows when he says good-bye to a class on a Friday, before moving on to the next point of call, whether he'll ever see those children again."

Fred Sloman

The school car families learned to live under the constant pressures of always being on the move. They accepted with grace the inevitable shoves and shunts that belong to railway living. Freight trains usually moved their school car from siding to siding.

Cela Sloman numbers over thirty crashes. The most severe crash came when a railroad worker at Foleyet turned the wrong switch and the engine came at full speed into their car. "We really broke things then," says Cela. "The Christmas cactus that was in bloom with a hundred blossoms was no longer."

The Slomans replaced their dishes with frequent regularity. Along with the other school car families, they praised the railway men who looked after them. "The trainmen were always good to us," says Cela. "They went out of their way to help." The passing freight trains delivered packages and letters. They dropped off extra grocery supplies and even buckets of coal to make sure the Baker heater had enough fuel. Cela remembers that when moving day came, the conductor walked into the school car. "He saw that there was a pillow at the baby's head in their little beds before they coupled."

The family never knew the exact time of the day or night when the freight would move them. The Board of Transport required that occupied railroad cars ride next to the caboose. Sometimes however, on a short run, the school car rode behind the engine. Whatever the hour of moving, the Slomans prepared themselves for the next ride.

Moving day held its own exact procedures. "The first thing we had to do was to take down the flagpole," says Margaret Sloman. They set up a ladder to reach the pole. It was attached into special clamps underneath the railcar. The family gathered inside all the toboggans, skis and sleds. The clothesline was taken down. They put anchors on the gas lamps so they wouldn't fall off the hooks on the ceiling. They checked the countertops to make sure they were cleared of any dishes. All the doors of the cupboards and the refrigerator were firmly shut. "If you didn't, you really could have a mess," laughs Margaret. The plants were put into the bathtub.

Often the school car families followed some of these precautions every night before they went to bed. A rough shunt could send a stray dish or flowerpot flying across the room. The school car family never knew if a train might come in the middle of the night and put a car off onto their siding.

At a teacher's convention someone asked

The Sloman school car is picked up in Capreol for another run.

school car teacher William Wright what he did for fun. Mr. Wright was stymied. "We lacked for very little in pleasure," he said. "We were isolated, but not lonely." He pointed out the beautiful landscapes, the unpolluted rivers that abounded in fish and the bush with wildlife. "We lacked very little," he said. "It seemed complete."

During World War II the teachers on the seven routes served about two hundred and fifty students each year. Then enrollment began to decline. More settlers came to the North. They established communities. Schools and highways (many former logging roads) were built. With the increasing number of roads, school busing began. By 1950 six school cars remained, but the enrollment had dropped to one hundred and forty students.

Change had come to the railroads as well. Diesel engines, electric signals and better railroad foundation beds for the tracks all helped to reduce the number of workers needed along the tracks. A section became twenty miles long. Telegraphers and their families moved away. The railroad men lived now in established towns and villages. Their children, who comprised the majority of Fred Sloman's students, looked no longer to the school car for their education.

The 1950s saw a slight increase in the number of school car students, about one hundred and sixty, but at the end of the decade the number dropped to one hundred.

The year 1967 brought the end to the school car. In the last two decades of operation Indian children began to replace the majority of students, once the children of railroad workers and other new Canadians. The school car had served Ukrainian, Polish, Spanish, Scandinavian, German and English children whose families had come North to log, mine and trap.

The education of Indian children belongs to federal jurisdiction. The government had often administered native education through private schools such as church institutions. But by the early 1960s most of the school car students came from native Indian families.

After Fred Sloman retired in 1965, only two school cars remained. Philip Fraser taught on the remaining Canadian National car that ran between Sioux Lookout and the Manitoba border. William Wright continued to conduct classes on CP's tracks from Chapleau to White River. The school car era came to an end when these two routes were disbanded. The cars went on display and toured the northern part of the province. The Canadian Pacific school car stands today in that railroad's museum in Delson, Quebec, a suburb of Montreal.

"If by chance I get to heaven after I put my chalk away, I will have only one request to make: two cheerful toots on an engine whistle please, when each old C. N. engineer comes through the gates after his final run."

Fred Sloman

Fred Sloman stayed on two years past his retirement to see that everyone of his students reached Grade 6. He felt that at this level they were equipped to handle correspondence courses. He estimated that over a thousand students went through his school car classes during his thirty-nine years of teaching.

Fred Sloman's school car retired when he did. His School-On-Wheels #15089 went to the North Bay railway shops of the Ontario Northland, the former Temiskaming and Northern Ontario Railroad. There the car was repainted. It was supposed to have stood at Expo '67 in Montreal or become part of the 1967 Centennial train that crossed Canada. "We were told to leave the schoolroom intact," says Cela. "That's why we left so many things behind." But the school car never took part in that year's nationwide celebrations.

Gerald Buck, who identified the school car as a former colonist car, has kept a watchful eye over #15089 in its retirement years. He believes it might have been put on display and possibly toured the North. It stayed close to the Northland yards, for at the time there was talk of a railroad museum in North Bay. When those plans never materialized, the Ontario Northland, in the late 1960s or early 1970s, gave the car to the Department of Education and the Ontario Science Centre. In Toronto it waited at the Canadian Pacific yards for the two groups to proceed with their plans to build a railroad museum or a transportation centre. That exhibition place was never constructed.

Fred Sloman lights a gasoline lamp that hangs from the ceiling. These two lamps shone far brighter than the coal oil lamps that stood along the car's walls. In the background hang the pictures of his children who have grown and left the school car for post secondary education.

- Robert C. Ragsdale

As a Grade 10 student at Runnymede Collegiate in 1969, Gerald Buck remembers seeing School Car #15089 from an overpass on his way to school. Every day he went by the West Toronto Canadian Pacific yards at Jane Street and St. Clair. It was during its stay there that a fire damaged some of its interior.

The car also stood at the CPR John Street yards in downtown Toronto. Mr. Buck, as well as his father, Frank, who worked there, saw the old car. It still contained some of its old school furnishings and artifacts. Mr. Buck thought the old car would be cut up for scrap.

The aging train however went to the Ontario Rail Association (ORA), an organization interested in railroad history and the restoration of old cars. Mr. Buck dates the year about 1970 or 1971. School Car #15089 remained with that organization for over a decade. Gerald Buck saw the car on the ORA siding at the Cawthra Road yards. It stood on tracks leased from the Department of Public Works.

After Fred Sloman's retirement in 1965, the family lost track of their former home and school. Cela and Fred moved to the family home in Clinton, Ontario, where Fred was born. His father, Jacob, had worked as a baggage master on the old Grand Trunk Railroad in the busy railroad town. Jacob Sloman built his house by hand on the corner of Matilda and Bond streets, in the design of a railroad station. It has a large front bay window similar to the telegraph operator's window that projects from the station building.

Fred and Cela grew up in Clinton, in southwestern Ontario's Huron County. They were childhood sweethearts. "I always knew Fred," recalls the former Cela Beacom. "I had red hair. That's why he liked me. Anything with red hair Fred liked. He told me the first time he saw me was when I sat on a big stool in my grandfather's grocery store."

They attended high school together. After Fred served overseas in World War I, he returned home with war injuries. He completed his education and taught at Blyth Continuation School, located ten miles from Clinton.

When he accepted a teaching position at Krugerdorf in Northern Ontario in 1923, he planned to return during Christmas week and marry Cela. "But he was stormstayed for several days," says Cela, "and he never arrived home until Christmas Eve. We were married at eleven o'clock that night."

Two years after Fred Sloman retired from teaching and returned to Clinton, he suffered a paralytic stroke on his left side. He was confined to a wheelchair and spent his last days in hospitals. He died in 1973.

Cela Sloman, now eighty-nine years old, continues to live with her daughter Margaret in the hundred-year-old home set among many tall trees. They both assumed their old school car was gone forever. Then one day a former school car student, Bill Stephenson, now a high-ranking Canadian National official in Edmonton, phoned the Slomans. He said he had read in a rail notice that Car Number 15089 was up for sale. Its cost was $2,000. The Slomans couldn't believe the news. They thought the fire-gutted car had long been consigned to its graveyard.

Mrs. Sloman and Margaret were determined to see the car. In August 1982 they drove to a private railroad salvage yard in Mississauga, west of Toronto. "The car was such a mess," says Margaret. "Only a shell was left." The gutted and stripped car seemed hopeless. "Everything had been removed," says Cela, "except the old bathtub and the furnace. They were too big to get out the door."

The Slomans recognized the car even though the name School-On-Wheels had been painted over. They would never forget the bathtub. They saw where the old drop-leaf table had been hinged. They recognized the unusual placement of the windows, for the old car had fewer and lower windows than the ordinary railroad car. And Margaret found the flagpole attached to its brackets underneath the car. "They probably didn't know what the pole was for, so they left it," she says.

The Slomans returned to Clinton and approached the town to buy the car. The railroad accepted their $1,500 offer. A volunteer committee was organized to help the Slomans bring back and restore the car.

On October 22 of that same year the battered old hulk arrived in Clinton.

Schoolchildren came to greet the car at the station. They held a banner that read "Coming Home to Clinton." They attached letters on the car's side that spelled "Welcome to Clinton." To celebrate the car's return, the Slomans and friends served railroad cake, a jelly roll-type cake that resmbled railroad tracks. A local bakery had made the white cake with raspberry filling.

"The car came on its own wheels," says Cela Sloman. "A slow freight brought it here." Ron Young, the chairman of the volunteer committee, boarded the train in Stratford, thirty-two miles away. He rode in the caboose, two cars behind the creaky School-On-Wheels. The nine-car train carried

Welcome to Clinton.   - Paul Wheeler

- Paul Wheeler

- Beacon Herald Photo

The old school car moves right smartly past the Sloman home on its way to its final stop at the Sloman Memorial Park. - Paul Wheeler

signs on both the school and the front of its engine. "C. N. takes School Car Home to Clinton Number 15089. October 22, 1982," they read.

At their own expense, the Slomans hired Fred Sole, a mover from Oil Springs, Ontario. He advertised that he could move anything. When the Slomans explained to him the enormous load they wanted him to move, he only nodded and said, "All things are possible."

He lived up to his advertising claim. He removed the wheels that weighed fifty-five tons, the bulk of the car's weight. With a crane he placed the railcar onto a flatbed truck. "The old train moved right smartly past our house," says Cela. It came to rest on the ties and rail bed already prepared for its arrival in the Sloman Memorial Park. Only five months earlier the town had named the park in his honour. The two acres on the Bayfield River had recently been created into a parkland. "It was supposed to be a quiet park by the river," says Margaret. "Just a place to come and sit."

The next two years saw the gradual restoration of the school car. With the help of volunteer labour and cash donations, the school half of the car was completed in 1984. A ceremony in July celebrated that restoration and commemorated the 70th year of the car's construction. "It was a birthday party," says Cela. The mayor, railroad and education representatives, and the federal and provincial members of Parliament attended. Hundreds of local students, former school car students and all of the Sloman children came to the celebration.

"We have no grants from the government," says Cela Sloman. "We're doing it on our own with private and individual donations." In 1985 the Masonic Lodge, of which Fred Sloman had been a long-time member, began to raise funds through its District Heritage Project. Eventually monies came from many other Masonic Lodge chapters throughout the province.

The restored school quarters has fifteen desks, more than the original number in the school car. "One desk came from as far away as Hamilton," says Margaret. The teacher's desk that stands at the front of the classroom came from the Canadian National Railway office in Goderich, located on Lake Huron, only twelve miles away.

The volunteer committee has tried to duplicate the original layout and fixtures of the car. The walls are painted beige. The brown-coloured, heavy-duty flooring replicates the original "battleship" linoleum.

Sliding blackboards run along the side. Another blackboard stands behind the teacher's desk. Shelving has been built in its original location. The coal oil lamps that stand in brackets on the wall have been electrified however. The Slomans have returned to the classroom some of Fred's old textbooks, his hand bell and the pointer for the roll-up maps.

The car now waits for the restoration of the living quarters. The volunteer committee hopes to complete the work by 1986. It will replace the fold-down table, the five bunk beds and restore the kitchen and bathroom. It will finish the replacement of the tongue-and-groove vertical siding on the exterior of the car. It is painted in the traditional brown-green of the old Canadian National railcars. "It was called Canadian National green," says Margaret, "and we needed twelve gallons."

Margaret Sloman, who worked many years as a homecare nurse for infants in Mothercraft, devotes full time to the car's restoration and maintenance. "She works ninety-eight hours a day," says her mother. Margaret has planted five thousand tulip bulbs in the flower gardens near the car. In 1985 she built her own low stone wall for wildflower plantings. She's the car's curator and tour leader. She escorts schoolchildren, Women's Institute members, senior citizen's groups, families, teachers and former school car students through the car. In 1985 her guest book registered more than eight hundred visitors.

In May 1986 Gerald Buck attended the unveiling ceremony of an Ontario historical plaque at the site of the School-On-Wheels in Clinton. He presented to Cela Sloman and her family several artifacts from the original car. One was a section of the ash door that had once stood at one end of the car. It has 15089 printed on it in gold. Mr. Buck also gave her three builder's plates from the rail car's "truck," the name given to the frame and wheels on which the beams of the car rest. The words "Crossen Car" were cast into the plates, but "Manufacturing" had been chiseled away. The deletion attests to the fact that the Cobourg, Ontario, Company was in the process of going out of rail car building.

Gerald Buck presented to Cela Sloman the nameplate from the huge stove she cooked on for thirty-nine years. And for an added reminder of her railroad years, she also received from him a window lifter or opener (a long wooden-handled device once used for prying open windows that became stuck and difficult to raise).

When Margaret walks the several blocks down the street from the family home to the school car, she runs the flag up the pole. It's her signal, just like that of her father, that the school car is open. It invites everyone to come aboard and relive the days when education offered new beginnings to the children of the North.

The Slomans, along with their many friends, are determined to see that the flag flies high above their school car once again. They want its lights to blaze out in the darkness and spread its own brightness just as it did for thirty-nine years.

When Cela Sloman sits at a school desk and looks out of the window, she's reminded of the North. Without any houses in view, and with only the bush and the Bayfield River flowing beyond, she recalls the North Country she loved.

In May of 1986 Gerald Buck, a member
of the Canadian Railroad Historical
Association, presented to Cela Sloman
several artifacts from the original school car
#15089.

Fred and Cela take a little time off
from the school car.

Schoolcar as it appears today.

School Car #15089 could find no more suitable place for its final stop. Its doors welcome visitors and retell the story of that romantic adventure in railroad history. It keeps alive the memory of that noble experiment, and it honours the dedication of its many selfless teachers, their wives and families. It also pays tribute to the many students who covered miles to seek out an education. One of its young pupils summed up his feelings in a prayer:

> Thank you God for the sun.
> Thank you for the blue sky
> and grass.
> But most of all, thank you
> for the school car.

Andrew Clement, North Bay, Ontario, compiled this list of school car teachers for his book, *The Bell and the Book,* scheduled for publication in the fall of 1986. Mr. Clement, now over 80 years old, recounts the story of his school car teaching days.

Teacher and School Car	Year Began	Length of Service
Fred Sloman Capreol West, C.N.	1926	40 years
Walter McNally Chapleau East, C.P.	1926	13 years
William Wright Chapleau West, C.P.	1928	40 years
William Fleming Port Arthur North Branch, C.N.	1928	18 Years * (approx.)
Andrew Clement Port Arthur West, C.N. Sioux Lookout West, C.N. North Bay North, C.N.R	1930	28 years
Angus and Helen McKay Sioux Lookout West, C.N. North Bay North, C.N.R	1934	12 years
Henry Antoniak Sioux Lookout West, C.N. Port Arthur West, C.N.	1938	10 years (approx.)
Cameron Bell Chapleau East, C.P.	1944	4 years
James Chalmers Port Arthur West, C.N.	1946	16 years
Philip Fraser Sioux Lookout West, C.N.	1946	19 years
Florence Bell Chapleau East, C.P.	1948	1 year
William Colcock Chapleau East, C.P.	1949	1 year
Cecil Corps Chapleau East, C.P.	1950	3 years

* Mr. Fleming was succeeded by the Englishman who burned down the school car accidently. The school car run never was started up again.